THE OFFICIAL
SUNDERLAND
ASSOCIATION
FOOTBALL CLUB ANNUAL 2007

**Written by Rob Mason, SAFC Publications Officer,
pages 56 & 57 by Barbara Mason.**

A Grange Publication

© 2006. Published by Grange Communications Ltd., Edinburgh, under licence from Sunderland Association Football Club. Printed in the EU.

Picture credits: Getty Images, Blades Sports Photography, Tony Carr, Martin Walker and Rob Mason. Thanks to Kenny McIver.

ISBN 1 905426 42 9

£6.99

CONTENTS

Niall Quinn is Sunderland's very special Chairman and manager. Niall used to be Sunderland's target man and what a player he was. When Kevin Phillips was winning the Golden Boot as Europe's top scorer it was Niall Quinn that was Superkev's partner and it was Niall who created so many of the chances that Phillips took so well. Not only that but Niall scored regularly himself: 69 in 183 starts for Sunderland.

When he retired in 2002 Niall was the all time leading goalscorer for his country, the Republic of Ireland, with 21 international goals. Just before the 2002 World Cup Niall organised a game between the Republic of Ireland and Sunderland at the Stadium of Light. It was a Benefit game for Quinn but he gave the £1m that was raised to charity, splitting it between hospitals in Sunderland and Dublin with an additional donation to a

NN

charity supporting poor children in India. That was another example of how special a person Niall is.

He first arrived on the football scene as a young striker with Arsenal, scoring against Liverpool on his league debut in 1985. After a few years with The Gunners he moved to Manchester City where he became a huge hero of City's excellent fans. Niall became the first Man City player for 20 years to score 20 goals in a season and added to his reputation by even going in goal in one game and saving a penalty!

In 1996 Quinn became Sunderland's record signing when the club paid £1.3m for him. In his early years at the club Niall was troubled by injury but he fought his way back to play some of the best football of his career as a veteran. Absolutely brilliant in the air, Niall was nobody's fool on the ground either and scored some of his greatest goals with his feet, one of the best being a delicate chip that completed the Stadium of Light's first ever hat trick against Stockport in 1998. Niall had

also scored the first ever goal at the Stadium of Light in 1997 against his old club Man City and now his aim is to take SAFC on what he described as a 'Magic carpet ride.'

Niall celebrates scoring away to Newcastle

STADIUM

The Stadium of Light has been Sunderland's home ground since 1997. It was the biggest football stadium built in England in the second half of the twentieth century and it has since been extended to its current capacity of 49,000.

When you walk into the stadium at ground level you are already at the back

OF LIGHT

of the first level of seats. This is because the pitch is lower than ground level and that is why the stadium seems bigger inside than it does from the outside.

As well as Sunderland games the stadium has hosted numerous important games including England internationals against Belgium and Turkey.

Take a TOUR

1 Guided tours of the Stadium of Light begin in the south west corner of the stadium just inside the tours entrance at turnstile number 4.

3 Imagine you are a player walking out of the players' tunnel. The classical music Sunderland run out to even gets played while you make your entrance!

2 Make sure you take the opportunity to sit in the manager's seat and pretend you are in control.

4 Have a look inside the dressing rooms and imagine your shirt hanging up there one day.

The Stadium of Light is a fantastic stadium. Coming to a game is brilliant but it's worth coming on a day when a game isn't on as well just to take a look behind the scenes. Every day of the year except Christmas Day you can come to the stadium and be taken on a guided tour that takes you right around the ground, into the dressing rooms, down the players' tunnel and you can even sit on the manager's seat in the dug out.

5

The Stadium of Light is built on an old coal mine called Wearmouth Colliery.
This banner from the pit hangs proudly in the West Stand.

7

Take a look at the pitch from one of the superb executive boxes.

6

You get to go in all of the big conference rooms and bars including the Sports Bar which is jam packed with memorabilia.

8

You will see the Centre of Light, SAFC's state of the art education block.
A Stadium Tour Certificate will be given to you at the end of the tour. To book a tour telephone 0191 551 5055.

GOALS, GOALS, GOALS

Whether it's a screamer from outside the box, a close range header, a team goal after a dozen passes, a brilliant free kick or a sloppy own goal, if it's a goal for the Lads then it's celebration time. When you come to the match it's goals that make your day. Crunching tackles and spectacular saves are all part of what makes up the beautiful game but it's goals that count!

13

THE ACADEMY of Light

Not only do Sunderland have one of the country's best stadiums in The Stadium of Light but the players also train at one of the best training grounds in the land. The Academy of Light is only a couple of miles from the stadium and it is a first class facility.

All of the club's players train there, from the youngest schoolboy coming in on an evening to the top players who on a Saturday will be running out at the stadium. Over the years Sunderland have produced some cracking players such as Michael Bridges who was sold for over £5m, England international Michael Gray, Scotland international Kevin Kyle and Northern Ireland International George McCartney. There are also people like Ben Alnwick, Chris Brown, Grant Leadbitter and Dan Smith in the first team squad for 2006-07 having come through the SAFC Academy system.

Ged McNamee is manager of the academy with Kevin Ball and Elliott Dickman as his assistants. This season's Under 18 players can be seen on pages 36 to 38.

As well as football pitches, the Academy of Light has superb facilities such as a gymnasium and swimming pools. Even the England team have used it to train when they've played in the north east!

SAFC

24-7 is the supporters' club for people who support Sunderland for 24 HOURS A DAY 7 DAYS A WEEK!

Some people support one club one month and another one another month depending who is the fashionable club at any time. That isn't proper support is it? Real football supporters support their team all the time.

Sunderland's supporters are as good as any. Sunderland supporters don't support the team some of the

time – they support Sunderland all of the time. That's why the junior supporters' club is called 24-7.

Being a 24-7 member gives you lots of things. For a start you get the 24-7 magazine which opens out into a massive poster and your special 24-7 bit of the safc.com website.

When you join you also get a gift box which has in it a SAFC autograph book, a bag and a pen.

24-7

What's more you get a 10% discount on SAFC Foundation soccer courses and 10% discount in the club shop at the Stadium of Light.

Probably best of all though is that you get an invitation to the 24-7 members' fun day. This is when you come to the Stadium of Light and have a go at things like football skills and penalty competitions, try the treasure hunt, make SAFC t-shirts and meet the two and only Samson and Delilah so you can get their 'paw-tographs.'

Now all of that should tell you that 24-7 is the purr-fect place for a Black Cat to be but what is more is that when you join 24-7 you are automatically entered into a competition to be a Sunderland mascot at the Stadium of Light. If you win that you won't just be a black cat – you'll be a top cat!

Give Samson a ring on 0191 551 5247 or log on to www.safc.com/247 and join the club. You will be very welcome.

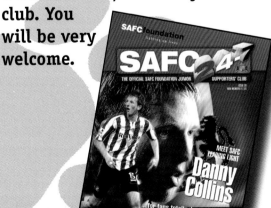

Summer SIGNINGS

KENNY CUNNINGHAM

Republic of Ireland international centre back Kenny Cunningham was Niall Quinn's first signing for Sunderland. Kenny is a vastly experienced player who is a great leader and organizer on the pitch.

Having begun is career in his native Ireland with Tolka Rovers, Cunningham started out in England with Millwall in the late 1980s, making over 100 appearances for them before becoming part of what was known as the 'Crazy Gang' at Wimbledon. Kenny spent eight seasons with the Dons playing exactly 250 league games for them before joining Birmingham in 2002. Voted 'Man of the Decade' at Birmingham, Kenny is now 35 and using his experience to help Sunderland back to the top.

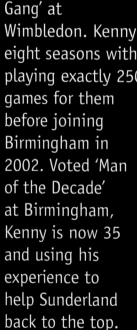

DARREN WARD

Goalkeeper Darren Ward is a Wales international who has played over 500 league games. He was signed at the beginning of the season after spending the last couple of years at Norwich City where he was reserve to England international Robert Green.

Before moving to Norwich, Darren had played all of his football in the Midlands where he kept goal for both Nottingham teams as well as his first club Mansfield.

Darren made his full debut for Wales away to Portugal in June 2000 and kept clean sheets in two of his five international games, the last coming in a 4-0 thumping of Scotland in 2004.

SUNDERLAND'S CREST

Sunderland have had their club badge since 1997. That was the year The Stadium of Light opened and the club decided to have a new badge as part of Sunderland's new start.

The main bit of the badge is split into four parts. The top left quarter shows an illustration of Penshaw Monument. This is a very well known local landmark which sits on the top of Penshaw Hill. People can see it from miles around and when supporters travel back from away games they know that they are nearly home when they can see Penshaw Monument in the distance. It is floodlit at night. Penshaw is on the outskirts of Sunderland and having it on the badge is a way of showing that Sunderland's support comes from much further afield than just the centre of Sunderland. In fact much of Sunderland's support is not from Sunderland itself but the old mining villages of County Durham.

In the bottom right corner of the main shield that is the main part of Sunderland's badge is a section of Wearmouth Bridge. This is the main bridge that links the north side of Sunderland with the south. The city centre is on the south side with the main shopping areas very close to the bridge. The Stadium of Light is just a couple of minutes' walk from the bridge on the north side of Sunderland. As with the inclusion of Penshaw Monument on the badge, having Wearmouth Bridge on it hints at Sunderland's support being widespread. The River Wear goes under the bridge and just up from it winds past the Stadium of Light carrying on right up into Weardale into the heartlands of Durham based support.

The other two sections of the shield show the club's famous colours of

CONSECTATIO EXCELLENTIAE

SUNDERLAND A.F.C

red and white stripes. If you add together all of the major trophies won by other English teams who wear red and white stripes (Southampton, Sheffield United, Stoke City, Lincoln City, Brentford, Cheltenham Town and Exeter City) they come to less than the six League Championships and two FA Cups won by Sunderland. In Spain Athletic Bilbao and Athletico Madrid's red and white striped kits stem from Sunderland's stripes.

The shield is held up by two black lions. These lions also feature on the City of Sunderland's coat of arms and having them on the club badge shows how closely linked the club are with the city. At the top of the badge is

a colliery winding gear wheel. The Stadium of Light stands on what was once Wearmouth Colliery, a coal mine that had seams running miles under the sea. Sunderland and County Durham were famous for coal mining and miners along with shipyard workers provided much of Sunderland's fantastic support over the years and so the colliery wheel recognises this and the fact the stadium stands on what was once the coalfield's biggest pit. There is also a replica colliery wheel outside the stadium.

The club motto 'Consectatio Excellentiae' at the top of the badge is Latin and means 'In Pursuit of Excellence.'

SUPER KEV (Kevin Phillips)

The only English player ever to win the Golden Boot as Europe's top scorer, SuperKev scored 30 Premiership goals for Sunderland in just 36 Premiership games in 1999-2000. Capped eight times by England, Phillips scored 130 goals in 235 games altogether for Sunderland and has also played for Watford, Southampton and Aston Villa.

CLOUGHIE (Brian Clough)

Famous as the manager who won the European Cup TWICE with Nottingham Forest and the League (now Premiership) with both Forest and Derby, Brian Clough was a brilliant goalscorer. No player has ever scored 250 league goals in as few games as Cloughie who began his career at Middlesbrough and then played for Sunderland. Unfortunately his career was cut short through injury. In the season he was injured he had scored 28 goals in just 28 games! Altogether he scored 251 goals in 274 league games!

SHACK (Len Shackleton)

Known as 'The Clown Prince of Soccer' Len Shackleton was one of the most skilful players the game has ever seen. Len was an inside forward or what we would now call an attacking midfield player. He was an outrageous player who would beat players near the corner flag by playing a 'one-two' with the flagpole. He'd tease defenders by looking like he'd mis-controlled the ball only to have put back spin on it so it came back to them and if he was bored he'd even sit on the ball to show how much time he had!

RAICH (Raich Carter)

Horatio Stratton Carter to give Raich his full name was Sunderland's captain when they won the FA Cup for the first time. He scored the second goal as Preston were beaten 3-1 at Wembley in 1937. A year earlier he'd scored 31 goals as Sunderland won the League. A brilliant passer of the ball, Raich Carter is arguably the greatest player ever to have played for Sunderland.

Why is Sunderland's THE Ground called...

STADIUM OF LIGHT?

Sunderland's 49,000 capacity ground is called The Stadium of Light as a tribute to the miners who traditionally have formed the bedrock of much of Sunderland's renowned support. The stadium is built on what was once Wearmouth Colliery, a coal mine which was one of the biggest in the country and the club's badge has a colliery winding gear wheel at the top.

This isn't the only reason the ground is called the Stadium of Light. The inventor of the incandescent electric light was from Sunderland. He was called Joseph Wilson Swan and Swan Street which is named after him is nearby. Furthermore the miners' safety lamp known as the Davy Lamp was invented by Sir Humphrey Davy at a pit in the Durham coalfield and a monument of a Davy Lamp shines permanently outside the stadium.

There are huge searchlights situated on the roof of the stadium and on a dark evening when they are switched on they sweep the Wearside skyline being visible for miles around.

Some people wrongly think that Sunderland's ground was named The Stadium of Light after the famous Portuguese club Benfica, whose ground is also called The Stadium of Light. The difference is that Benfica's ground is officially called The Estadio do Sport Lisboa e Benfica but is nicknamed The Stadium of Light because it is situated in an area called Luz which in Portuguese means Light. It is a similar thing to the ground shared by AC Milan and Internazionale of Milan. Their famous Stadium is really called the Giuseppe Meazza Stadium but it is commonly known as the San Siro.

At Sunderland though the Stadium of Light is not a nickname, nor is it connected to the area the ground is in, which is called Monkwearmouth. Instead the name pays tribute to the people who worked on or under the site in years gone by, people who worked in the mining industry at all, the role Sunderland and Durham have played in the invention of incandescent electric light and Davy Lamps and perhaps most of all because it illuminates the way forward for the club and its supporters.

Why are Sunderland called the... BLACK CATS?

Sunderland's nickname is The Black Cats. Black cats are thought by many people to be lucky. Sunderland are first known to have had a black cat as a lucky mascot over 100 years ago. In 1905 the chairman of the time, Mr. F.W. Taylor, was pictured in a cartoon with a black cat sat on a football. In 1913 when Sunderland got to the FA Cup Final for the first time Sunderland supporters wore little black cat badges.

In the 1930s Sunderland's programmes had a black cat on the cover and when Sunderland won the FA Cup for the first time in 1937 a twelve year old supporter at the match called Billy Morris was found to have kept a black kitten (with red and white ribbons) in his pocket throughout the match.

Sunderland AFC Supporters' Association have always had a black cat as their emblem since they were formed in 1965 and in the year 2000 Sunderland officially adopted the nickname The Black Cats, a year after the first team strip had had a black cat emblem on the sleeve. The club's mascots Samson and Delilah are also black cats.

The football club was formed in 1879 but in fact the idea of linking black cats with Sunderland goes back all the way to 1805! Sunderland is on the coast and at the harbour there were gun batteries to guard against attack. One famous night a volunteer from the Sunderland Loyal Volunteers heard such an ear piercing wailing he thought it came from the devil himself! However when the soldiers went to search for where the noise was coming from it was found to be coming from a black cat and after that the gun battery became known as the Black Cat Battery. This was at Roker where Sunderland played for many years.

Stokoe's STATUE

One of SAFC's greatest ever days came on May 5th 1973. That was the day of one of the most sensational FA Cup Finals of all time. Sunderland were in the Second Division (what is now called The Championship) and were playing Leeds United.

At that time Leeds was one of the best teams in Europe. They had won the FA Cup the year before, they had a European Final to play later the same month and a year later they would win the League. Their team included some of the top stars of the day, people like Billy Bremner, Johnny Giles, Norman Hunter Allan Clarke, Eddie Gray and Peter Lorimer.

Sunderland in comparison had been near the bottom of the Second Division

six months earlier when Bob Stokoe took over as manager. He had transformed the team. Top First Division sides Manchester City and Arsenal had been well beaten on the way to the Cup Final and Sunderland was gripped by FA Cup fever.

Nonetheless Leeds were the hottest favourites for years and years to win the cup but Stokoe's Stars, as his team became known, won 1-0. Ian Porterfield scored the all important goal and goalkeeper Jimmy

Montgomery made the greatest save ever made in a Cup Final to ensure Sunderland won the cup.

At the final whistle Bob Stokoe ran across the pitch to goalkeeper Montgomery and that moment has been brilliantly captured in this statue of Stokoe that was put up outside the Stadium of Light in July.

Stokoe became known as 'The Messiah' in Sunderland and whenever you go to the Stadium of Light and see Stokoe's statue you'll know just why he deserves to be remembered forever.

Bob Stokoe's statue with four members of the 1973 FA Cup winning team and Bob's daughter Karen. Left to right: Ritchie Pitt, Bobby Kerr, Karen Craven, Dick Malone and Jimmy Montgomery.

SPOT THE DIFFERENCE

Can you spot the differences between these two pictures of Sunderland against Manchester United? There are ten to find.

RED & WHITE BEDROOMS

Is your bedroom a red and white bedroom? Walk into the rooms of some supporters and straight away you are left in no doubt about who they support.

Sometimes people decorate their bedrooms in honour of a particular singer or film star but favourite bands and movies tend to change whereas if you support Sunderland they are your team for life.

Some fans plaster their walls with pictures of Sunderland players from the match programme, some make sure they have Sunderland curtains, bedspreads, pillow cases, slippers, dressing gowns and so on. In fact you name it someone has it in red and white and in a room like this you can see that the owner eats, breathes and sleeps SAFC!

Promotion CHASE

Throw a three to get three points to begin your season by moving to number three.

1

2

3

You lose an early season game against a newly promoted side. Miss a turn.

4

Your big new signing is injured and ruled out for six weeks. Go back to number one.

5

You sign a top class striker just before the transfer window closes. Have an extra turn.

6

7

8

Your no 9 scores a hat trick, move forward 3 spaces.

9

10

A last minute penalty causes you to lose a game you really should have won. Go back one space.

11

12

You have no luck in an important game. Miss a turn.

13

Two of your best players recover from injury in time for a match. Move forward one space.

14

15

16

Name five past or present SAFC goalies for an extra throw.

17

You give a 17 year old his debut and he scores. Move forward two spaces.

18

19

20

You have three players sent off in one game. Miss a turn.

21

22

You give away a last minute pena with the score 0-0. the person who is on right can name ten Sund players in 30 seconds yo to go back four spac

23

To play this game you will need a dice and counters for each player. You can have as many players as you like. Move forward one space for every number you throw, eg, if you throw a 4, move forward 4 spaces. Follow the instructions on the number and see if you can win the promotion race. The winner is the first person to reach number 46.

24

You begin a run of four defeats in a row. Go back to number 28.
35

Suspensions pile up, miss a turn.
36

If you are first to number 46 you have won the league, Well done!
46

You play your nearest challengers. Roll the dice twice. The first is your opponent's score and the second roll is your score. Win and go forward three spaces, lose and go back three. Draw and don't move.
25

34

You achieve a vital win, have an extra go.
37

45

The teams above you all lose, move forward two spaces.
26

33

38

Your nearest rivals win their game in hand, miss a turn.
44

You have a spate of injuries, miss a turn.
27

32

Fixture problems pile up, miss a turn.
39

43

28

31

40

Your goalkeeper is injured on international duty, miss a turn.
42

29

Your striker is clean through in the last minute with the scores level. Roll the dice and if you get a 4,5 or 6 you've scored and can move forward an extra three spaces.
30

A dodgy decision costs you points, go back to number 38.
41

GREAT

Jimmy Montgomery

Goalkeeper Jimmy Montgomery played many more games for Sunderland than anyone else ever has done - 627 in all. Monty made brilliant reaction saves week in week out and one of his best came in the 1973 FA Cup Final when second division (what is now called The Championship) Sunderland sensationally beat Leeds United who at that time were the top team in the country. Sunderland won 1-0 with a goal from Ian Porterfield but the game is most famous for Monty's double save from Trevor Cherry and Peter Lorimer. It was undoubtedly the greatest save ever made at Wembley Stadium.

Chris Turner

Not very big for a goalkeeper at only 5'10", Chris Turner was a fantastic goalie. He played for Sunderland between 1979 and 1985 when he was transferred to Manchester United. In his last season at Sunderland, Turner took Sunderland to Wembley with a series of brilliant displays in the League Cup and he was only beaten at Wembley by a deflected goal as Sunderland lost 1-0 to Norwich City.

GOALIES

Thomas Sorensen

Denmark international Thomas won more caps as an international goalkeeper while on Sunderland's books than all of the club's previous goalkeepers put together! In 2002 he also became the first goalkeeper to play in the World Cup Finals while with Sunderland. A terrific all round goalkeeper who could dominate his box, Sorensen secured his legendary status at Sunderland by saving an Alan Shearer penalty away to Newcastle in 2000. Shearer's late penalty gave the Magpies the chance to draw the derby match but Thomas' save meant Sunderland won.

Mart Poom

'The Poominator' didn't just stop goals for Sunderland – he scored them! The only goalie ever to score a (competitive) goal for Sunderland, the vastly experienced Estonian international once scored with a stunning last minute header away to his previous club Derby County. It was as good a header as you will ever see. Mart was also a fantastic goalkeeper, he could make point blank saves and come to the edge of his box to take crosses. In 2006 he won a Champions League runners up medal as a sub for Arsenal.

Every club needs to produce their own players. Sunderland's Academy has produced some good footballers over the years such as England international Michael Gray who is now at Blackburn Rovers, Michael Bridges who was sold for over £5m and full internationals George McCartney and Kevin Kyle who have been important players for Sunderland in recent years.

Sunderland has an Under 18 team that play Academy matches at The Academy of Light. The players in this team have already done very well to be signed by a professional club and all will be hoping to progress in the game and go on to have careers as professional footballers. Of course only a few ever do so at any club because the standard gets higher and higher the older you get. If you look at any old youth team photograph from any club you'll see that most of the players have not progressed as they would have hoped but you can also spot players who are now famous who were once playing youth team football and hoping to stand out and go on to become a success.

Dave Dowson

England international striker from Bishop Auckland in County Durham. He has been at the club since he was twelve and is a hard working player who can finish well. Scored a hat trick in the FA Youth Cup last season.

Jordan Henderson

A stylish creative midfielder or striker from East Herrington in Sunderland. Jordan made his U18 debut in April 2006. Born June 17th 1990.

Joshua Home-Jackson

A striker from Easington Village, Josh was born on December 30th 1989 and made his U18 debut as a sub in a 3-2 win over Manchester United in April 2006.

ONES

The lads at Sunderland hoping to become successes of the future

Jordan Cook

Local lad from Easington Lane. Jordan plays up front off the main striker and has been with Sunderland since he was seven.

Chris Backhouse

Wakefield born goalkeeper who has previously played for Manchester United and Leeds. Chris has been with Sunderland since the summer of 2005. Born December 13th 1988.

Jack Colback

A midfielder from Killingworth near Newcastle, Jack was born on October 24th 1989 and began to break into the Sunderland team last season while he was still at school.

Jamie Chandler

England international midfielder from Boldon near Sunderland. Jamie tackles well and has a good range of passing. Born March 24th 1989.

Lee Chapman

Seaham born striker who made his debut at Middlesbrough's Riverside Stadium in the FA Youth Cup in January 2005 and scored on his U18 league debut a few days later. Born March 12th 1989.

Gavin Donoghue

Republic of Ireland youth international defender who is physically commanding. Born March 3rd 1988.

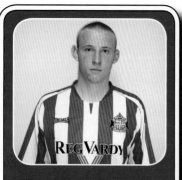

Liam Connolly

Left back or left sided central defender from Jarrow, born September 8th 1988.

Michael Kay

England youth international centre back from Consett in County Durham. Michael is a strong defender who can use the ball well. Born September 12th 1989.

Richard Smith

Giant centre back who would be the man to mark Peter Crouch! Born March 20th 1989 and from Durham.

Michael Liddle

A Republic of Ireland U18 international left back. Made his Sunderland U18 debut against Manchester United in January 2006. Born in Haydon Bridge in Northumberland on September 12th 1989.

Nathan Luscombe

Nathan can play at left back or on the left side of midfield. He makes forceful runs forward and has great determination. Born November 6th 1989 in Harlow Green Gateshead.

Niall McArdle

A centre back from the Republic of Ireland. Niall made his first appearances for the club in a tournament in France at Easter 2006. Born March 22nd 1990 in Malahide in County Dublin.

Robbie Weir

Northern Ireland youth international midfielder who can also play up front. Robert played in a senior league in Ireland for Larne before coming to Sunderland. Born December 9th 1988.

Martyn Waghorn

Martyn is a striker who can also play on the left side of midfield. He possesses a powerful shot and did well to make a first appearance at Reserve team level when he was only 15 and played away to Liverpool. Born January 23rd 1990, Martyn comes from South Shields.

SAMSON and DELILAH

Samson and Delilah are Sunderland's mascots. These black cats are Sunderland's top cats. They entertain the fans before every home game and sometimes travel to away games too. Both of them have their birthdays on July 24th because that is the 24th of the 7th and they are the couple who run Sunderland's junior supporters' club 24-7. Samson and Delilah look after the mascots at the game, often turn up at presentations organised by Sunderland's charity, the SAFC Foundation and Samson even has his own column in the local sports paper, 'The Football Echo.' Before you begin to think Samson and Delilah are purr-fect though, you should realise that from time to time they have been known to be a bit cheeky especially when they've met up with the mascots of visiting teams or visiting supporters having a go at the half time penalty shoot out. It's all good fun though and if you come to the Stadium of Light look out for Samson and Delilah before the match and at half time.

GLOBAL GAME

REPUBLIC OF IRELAND - STEPHEN ELLIOTT

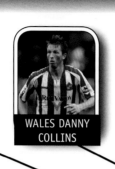

WALES DANNY COLLINS

NORTHERN IRELAND - GEORGE MCCARTNEY

SCOTLAND - KEVIN KYLE

DENMARK - THOMAS SORENSEN

AMERICA - CLAUDIO REYNA

BRAZIL - EMERSON THOME

MOROCCO - TALAL EL KARKOURI

ARGENTINA - JULIO ARCA

ZAMBIA - JEFF WHITLEY

SOUTH AFRICA - DON KICHENBRAND (50S FORWARD)

See where Sunderland players of the past and present were born

ENGLAND - JON STEAD

FRANCE - ERIC ROY

SWEDEN - STEFAN SCHWARZ

AUSTRIA - JURGEN MACHO

NORWAY - THOMAS MYHRE

ESTONIA - MART POOM

POLAND - DARIUSZ KUBICKI

SLOVAKIA - STANISLAV VARGA

SWITZERLAND - BERNT HAAS

SINGAPORE - TERRY BUTCHER

AUSTRALIA - WILLIE FRASER (50S GOALIE)

KENYA - IAIN HESFORD

CAMEROON - PATRICK MBOMA

GERMANY - THOMAS HELMER

HOLLAND - EDWIN ZOETEBIER

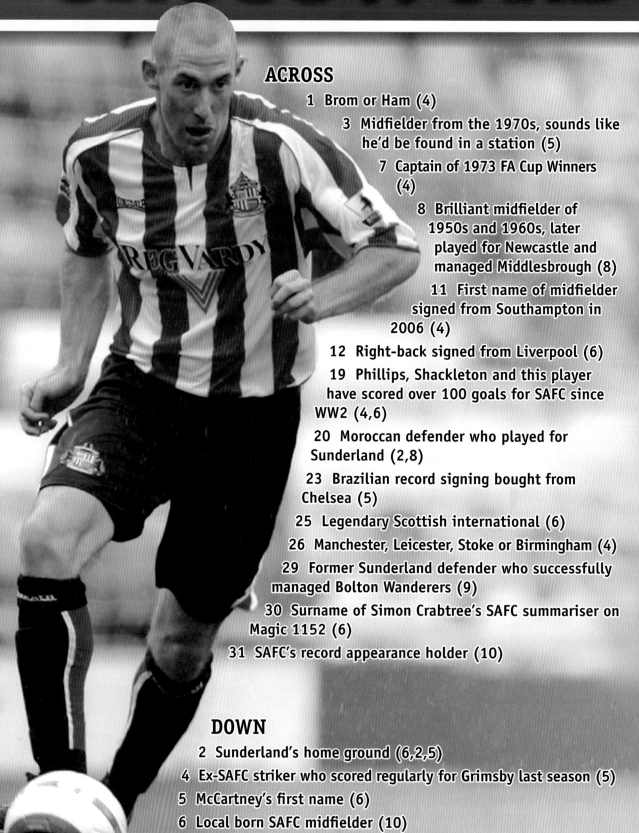

CROSSWORD

ACROSS

1 Brom or Ham (4)

3 Midfielder from the 1970s, sounds like he'd be found in a station (5)

7 Captain of 1973 FA Cup Winners (4)

8 Brilliant midfielder of 1950s and 1960s, later played for Newcastle and managed Middlesbrough (8)

11 First name of midfielder signed from Southampton in 2006 (4)

12 Right-back signed from Liverpool (6)

19 Phillips, Shackleton and this player have scored over 100 goals for SAFC since WW2 (4,6)

20 Moroccan defender who played for Sunderland (2,8)

23 Brazilian record signing bought from Chelsea (5)

25 Legendary Scottish international (6)

26 Manchester, Leicester, Stoke or Birmingham (4)

29 Former Sunderland defender who successfully managed Bolton Wanderers (9)

30 Surname of Simon Crabtree's SAFC summariser on Magic 1152 (6)

31 SAFC's record appearance holder (10)

DOWN

2 Sunderland's home ground (6,2,5)

4 Ex-SAFC striker who scored regularly for Grimsby last season (5)

5 McCartney's first name (6)

6 Local born SAFC midfielder (10)

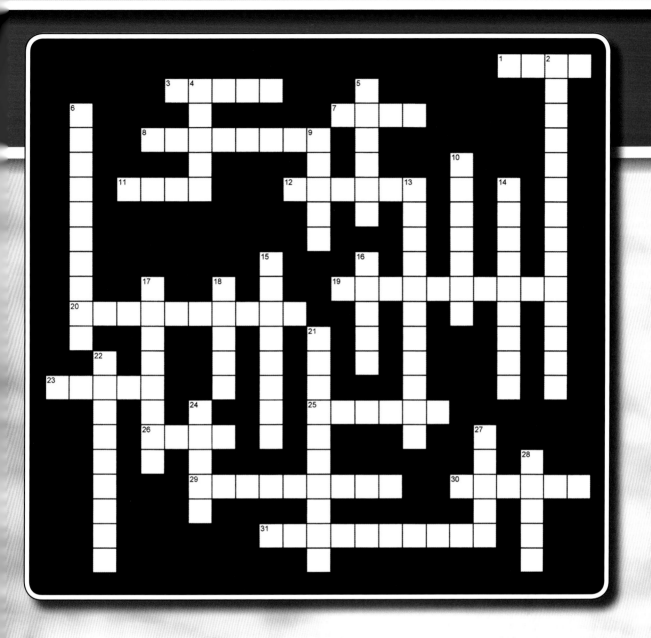

9   First name of right-back signed from Gillingham (5)

10 Team Jon Stead scored his first Sunderland goal against (7)

13 Midfielder signed from Ipswich in 2005 (5,6)

14 Midfielder signed from Oxford (9)

15 Goalkeeper who scored for Sunderland away to Derby (4,4)

16 First name of exciting striker with Italian sounding name of 8 down (5)

17 Midfielder whose 2006 goal at Fulham was named as Match of the Day's 'Goal of the Month' (8)

18 Substitute in the 1973 FA Cup Final, he's not old (5)

21 Exciting forward with Italian sounding name (10)

22 Surname of SAFC's ex-Gillingham right-back, see 7 down (9)

24 Began with Huddersfield, signed for SAFC from Blackburn (5)

27 What you suffer if you lose an important game (5)

28 Collins but not Danny (5)

GREAT

SUNDERLAND 4-1 CHELSEA, December 4th 1999 Premiership

Seven minutes to go to half time and you are 4-0 up having ripped to shreds an all star Chelsea team including Zola, Desailly, Terry, Poyet, Wise and Flo.
The golden years of Kevin Phillips and Niall Quinn are summed up by this game. Each of them scored twice. The Londoners pulled a consolation goal back late on but on this day Sunderland would have beaten any team on the planet.

SUNDERLAND 2-2 MANCHESTER United, December 28th 1999, Premiership

Despite missing Super Kevin Phillips, Sunderland raced into a 2-0 lead in this top of the table clash through goals from Gavin McCann (*right*) and Niall Quinn. The quality of the football from both sides was superb with Roy Keane at his best as he hauled United back into the match with an inspirational performance and a quality goal but the visitors still needed a fortunate goal from a late free kick to claim a draw.

SUNDERLAND 4-4 CHARLTON ATHLETIC (6-7 on penalties) May 25th 1998, Play Off Final

Sunderland fans had ten goals to cheer but still ended up losing. The Play Off Final is an incredibly important game and this was as dramatic as any. The lead changed hands several times as the 90 minutes ended with the score at 3-3. Each team scored once more in extra time before the place in the Premiership came down to penalties. You rarely see a team score all five of its penalties in a shoot out but Sunderland managed six out of six. Charlton though were just as good from the spot and when they scored their seventh they won the game after Sunderland's Michael Gray saw his shot saved by Sasa Illic. It was massively disappointing but it was still one of the greatest games ever seen at Wembley.

GAMES

SUNDERLAND 2-1 CHELSEA, March 18th 1992
FA Cup 6th Round Replay

A place in the FA Cup semi final was the reward for the winners of this match. Sunderland had drawn 1-1 at Stamford Bridge to earn this replay and had taken the lead through Peter Davenport after which Chelsea had put the lads under more and more pressure. Sunderland 'keeper Tony Norman made some fantastic saves but was at last beaten just four minutes from the end. It looked as if Chelsea would go on and win in extra time as they'd been the stronger team but from a last minute corner midfielder Gordon Armstrong (*below*) scored with an amazing header from just inside the penalty area. The scenes of celebration were some of the wildest Roker Park ever saw.

SUNDERLAND 3-1 MANCHESTER CITY, February 27th 1973
FA Cup 5th Round Replay

When Sunderland's former ground Roker Park closed in 1997 after 99 years, this was the match that supporters voted as the best. Manchester City were the cup favourites, Bob Stokoe hadn't long been in charge at Sunderland but had seen his team earn a 2-2 draw at Man City to set up this replay. City were still red hot favourites but Sunderland destroyed them even though City tried to come back in the second half. Two goals from Billy Hughes and a thunderbolt shot from Vic Halom (*below*) capped a brilliant performance.

CAN YOU WIN PROMOTION?

There are 25 questions for you here worth a point each. The answers are on page 61. If you can get 20 – 23 questions right you are good enough for automatic promotion. If you are really brilliant and get 24 or 25 right then you win the Championship. If you get between 15 and 19 correct then you face the dreaded Play Offs so just in case you end up in the Play Off zone try the Play Off questions before you look at the answers.

GROUNDS
1) What is Sunderland's ground called?
2) What was the name of Sunderland's home ground in 1997 before they moved to their current ground?
3) What is the name of Liverpool's ground?
4) What is the name of Derby County's ground?
5) What is the name of Barcelona's ground?

NICKNAMES
1) What is Sunderland's nickname?
2) Which team who play in red and white stripes are nicknamed 'The Blades'?
3) Who are The Gunners?
4) Who are The Toffees?
5) Who are The Saints?

GOALIES

1) Who did Sunderland sign Kelvin Davis from?
2) Who was Sunderland's goalie when they won the FA Cup in 1973?
3) Which country does Man Utd's Edwin van der Sar play for?
4) Which goalie once scored for Sunderland at Derby?
5) Which Premiership goalie plays for an international team that sounds like his own name?

STRIKERS

1) Which Sunderland striker's dad also played for Sunderland?
2) Which Sunderland striker scored against Newcastle and Manchester United last season?
3) Which teenage Arsenal striker was in England's World Cup squad?
4) Which former Sunderland striker is the only English player ever to win the European Golden Boot, the prize for Europe's top scorer?
5) Which striker did Sunderland have on loan from Liverpool all last season?

TRANSFERS

Match these players up with the clubs Sunderland signed them from:

Rory Delap	Blackburn Rovers
Stephen Wright	Gillingham
Dean Whitehead	Liverpool
Nyron Nosworthy	Southampton
Jon Stead	Oxford United

PLAY OFF QUESTIONS

Try these in case you end up with between 15 and 19 points and finish in the Play Off Zone. You have to get the semi final question correct for your Final answer to count. If you get both right then you win promotion.

PLAY OFF SEMI FINAL QUESTION

Who was Sunderland's manager when Sunderland lost to Crystal Palace in the Play Offs in 2004?

PLAY OFF FINAL QUESTION

Who did Sunderland play in the 1998 Play Off Final at Wembley in 1998 when the teams drew 4-4 before Sunderland lost 7-6 on penalties? (*See above.*)

SUNDERLAND
On the Web

safc.com is Sunderland's website. It is the place to go to keep up to date with everything that is happening at the club.

The website delivers all the news on a daily basis. Whether it's news from the manager, the players, ticket news, match news, injury news – it's all there.

You can get live commentary on every Sunderland game, match reports during and after games and reaction quicker than anywhere else. By visiting safc.com you won't miss any of the action.

The players read the website and they answer your questions in our exclusive webchats and Q&A sessions. How cool is that?

There are also lots of fun and games to be had in our 24-7 section; and our fanzone section is full of stuff to see and do. You can even write for safc.com!

If you visit SAFC World, the video and audio service of the club's official website, you can get exclusive video interviews with the players and manager and see all of the goals.

Not only that but if you want to buy anything such as tickets, strips, programmes, T-shirts etc you can do so online through our online store.

There are over 81 million websites in the world ... but only one if you are a big Sunderland fan.

Visit safc.com every day

Player PROFILES

BEN ALNWICK
Excellent goalkeeper who will be 20 on New Year's Day 2007. Sunderland won promotion on the day Ben made his debut in 2005 and in his second match the Championship was won with a 2-1 win at West Ham when Ben made a save from Marlon Harewood that was voted the 'save of the season.' He had five games in the Premiership in 2005-06 and made a brilliant full length penalty save from Tottenham's Robbie Keane at White Hart Lane.

TREVOR CARSON
Highly rated Northern Ireland youth international goalkeeper who has occasionally played up front for the academy side! Has been on the bench for the first team but at the start of this season was still to make his debut.

KEVIN SMITH
Young striker signed from Leeds mid way through last season. Scored six goals in his first eight starts for the reserves including a hat trick against West Brom. At the start of this season was still to make his first team debut.

STEPHEN WRIGHT

A right back who cost £3.5m from Liverpool in 2002 but missed almost all of the 2005-06 season through injury. A former England Under 21 international, Stephen once scored against Jens Lehmann in the Champions League and won a 'man of the match' award in a star studded game between Manchester United and Liverpool. His dad, John, is a masseur at Anfield.

STEVE CALDWELL

A fantastic professional. Scotland international Steve is a wholehearted player who never gives anything less than 100%. The scorer of the goal that sealed Sunderland's promotion in 2005, the centre back began his career with Newcastle and also played on loan to Leeds before coming to Sunderland. His brother Gary is also a Scotland international.

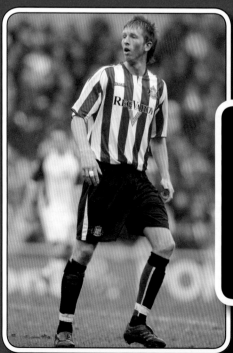

DANNY COLLINS

Danny has played football and cricket for Wales and has also represented England at football at semi professional level when he was with his home city Chester. A centre back who can also play at left back, Danny began his career as a midfield player but was converted into a centre back by former England centre back Mark Wright when he was his manager at Chester.

NEILL COLLINS

Scotland Under 21 international who played for Queens Park and Dumbarton before signing for Sunderland. Since he has been at the Stadium of Light he has been out on loan to Hartlepool United and Sheffield United.

NYRON NOSWORTHY

A firm favourite with many Sunderland fans, Nyron or 'Nugsy' as he is nicknamed, has established his place in the hearts of supporters through his non stop effort and commitment. A player with strength and pace, Nyron sometimes makes simple mistakes but his attitude can't be faulted. Before coming to the north east he played 199 times for Gillingham.

PETER HARTLEY

Young central defender in his first season as a professional. Can also play at left back but prefers central defence. Strong in the air and likes to hit long diagonal passes.

TOMMY MILLER

Made his name as a goalscoring midfielder with Hartlepool and Ipswich before coming to Sunderland in 2005. Twice the top scorer for Hartlepool, Tommy was selected for the PFA Championship team of the season in his last year at Ipswich and scored three times in his first season at Sunderland. Although born in the north east he qualifies to play for Scotland but had to withdraw through injury when selected for Scotland's international squad.

LIAM LAWRENCE

Attacking midfielder who joined Sunderland from Mansfield and has done well enough to force himself into the Republic of Ireland international set up. Nicknamed 'Lennie' Lawrence can score some spectacular goals and two of his best came last season. He scored with a stunning shot away to Newcastle and then won BBC TV's 'Goal of the Month' competition for a left foot volley away to Fulham.

DEAN WHITEHEAD

Deano has won Player of the Year Awards in each of the last three seasons. Currently Sunderland's 'Player of the Year', he was Sunderland's 'Players' Player of the Year' a season earlier when Sunderland won the Championship and in 2003-04 he was Player of the Year at his previous club Oxford United when he was also named by the PFA in their divisional XI for the season. A hard working midfielder who likes to take free kicks, his best moment in the Premiership came when he beat England goalkeeper Paul Robinson with a thirty yard free kick away to Spurs.

ANDY WELSH

An exciting left winger who has a speedy turn of pace and can cross on the run. A Scotland U19 international, Andy was plucked from Stockport County and did well in his first few months at the Stadium of Light. He added to his experience with a successful loan spell at Leicester City but returned to Sunderland to gain more Premiership experience under caretaker manager Kevin Ball.

GRANT LEADBITTER

Midfielder who has gained a lot of international experience at junior levels for England. Went on loan to Rotherham United in 2005 to gain league experience and ended Sunderland's Premiership campaign in 2006 by beginning to force himself into Sunderland's starting line up. Has the ability to tackle and shoot in addition to a good range of passing.

JONATHAN STEAD

Former Huddersfield, Blackburn and England U21 striker who cost £1.8m. Started this season with 31 league and cup goals to his name. Has quick feet and is able to drop into midfield to get involved in build up play.

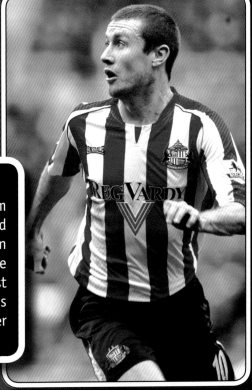

STEPHEN ELLIOTT

Republic of Ireland international striker. Signed from Manchester City in the summer of 2004, he scored sixteen goals in his first season as Sunderland won promotion. Stephen was getting to grips with life in the Premiership, scoring great goals against Manchester United and Newcastle but then was restricted by injury problems. Elliott is a cool finisher with plenty of pace.

KEVIN KYLE

Scotland international target man who has fought his way back after a long term hip injury that saw him travel the world in search of a cure. Kevin scored 16 goals in the 2003-04 season before injuries put his career on hold. Kyle is a powerful forward who is physically very tough. He can be a nightmare for defenders to try and mark.

CHRIS BROWN

The son of former Sunderland striker Alan Brown, Chris grew up as a Sunderland supporter and has represented England up to Under 20 level. He began his career on loan to his home town team Doncaster with whom he won a League Two medal in 2004 before adding a Championship medal with Sunderland a year later. Chris has also had a spell on loan to Hull City.

DARYL MURPHY

A Republic of Ireland Under 21 international forward whose first goal for Sunderland was a dramatic last minute equaliser against Spurs in the Premiership. Once with Luton as a teenager, Daryl returned to Ireland and joined Sunderland for £100,000 in 2005 after a terrific season with Waterford. He had a spell on loan to Sheffield Wednesday in his first year with Sunderland where he has often played on the left of midfield as well as up front.

Fan-TASTIC

Sunderland supporters are right up there with the very best. The noise that pours down from the stands at the Stadium of Light can be awesome. At Sunderland's old ground Roker Park it was known as the Roker Roar, while now the Stadium of Light can be turned into the Stadium of Sound.

Any team's supporters can make plenty of noise when their team is winning of course. That's easy and Sunderland supporters like to win as much as any club's fans do but when things aren't going well and the team are having a bad time the red and white legions still know how to lift a team by getting right behind them, urging them on and simply being 'fan-tastic'.

Sunderland fans are well known for having lots of songs. At some clubs there are a handful of songs that are relied upon but Sunderland seem to have a lot of songs. Some of them can be a bit rude of course especially when they are about a team that play not far away from Sunderland so we won't include any of the rude ones in our SAFC Top Five:

Wise Men Say
'Wear' On Our Way
My Garden Shed
Niall Quinn's Disco Pants
Come On Nyron

Samson sho

You will need: 200 gm self raising flour
- **200 gm caster sugar**
- **200 gm soft margarine/butter**
- **4 eggs**
- **1/2 teaspoon vanilla essence**
- **250 gm ready to roll white icing**
- **50 gm ready to roll black icing**
- **1 tube red writing icing**

You will also need a 22.5 cm cake tin greased with butter, a rolling pin and a little icing sugar to use for rolling out the icing. Before you start, set your oven to 180°c/350°f/Gas 4 and WASH YOUR PAWS!!

1: Put the butter and sugar in a large mixing bowl and beat together with a wooden spoon until the mixture is pale and fluffy.

2: Stir in the beaten eggs, vanilla essence and flour and gently mix together. Spoon the mixture into the tin and smooth the top.

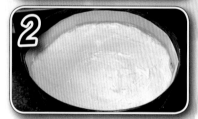

3: Bake for 65–70 minutes. Take out of the oven and leave to cool for a few minutes before turning the cake out onto a rack until completely cold.

4: Sprinkle a little icing sugar onto a board and the rolling pin and roll out the white icing to a 22.5 cm circle (use a plate or your cake tin as a guide). Also roll out the black icing to a 8 X 14 cm rectangle.

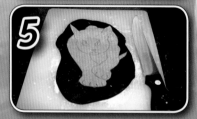

5: Lay the white icing circle on top of the cold cake and press it down gently. Trace the outline of the black cat (bottom right) onto tracing paper and cut out. Lay this on the black icing and cut round the shape with a sharp knife.

6: Stick the black cat in the centre of the cake with a few drops of water. Draw the lines on the cat with the writing icing to put the details on. Write HAPPY BIRTHDAY with the icing on the cake.

MATCHDAY

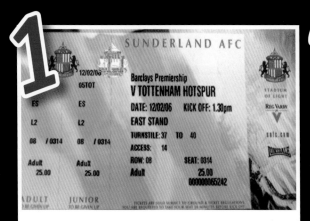

BUY A TICKET

You can get a ticket in advance by ringing the ticket office on 0845 671 1973, Ticketmaster on 08705 862 015, calling in to the ticket office at the Stadium of Light or online from safc.com. If the game is not sold out you can usually pay cash on the day of the game.

GET TO THE STADIUM

You can get a metro to the Stadium (Get off at the Stadium of Light station or St. Peter's station), walk across from Sunderland City Centre or get a lift to the ground although parking can be difficult. SAFC have a great Park and Ride system where the person bringing you can park their car a mile or two from the stadium and then take a bus to and from the ground.

BEFORE THE MATCH

Stewards will point you to your seat if you ask them. Once you are there you can read your programme, watch the pre-match entertainment, look out for the mascots Samson and Delilah or go and get a drink or something to eat. All of the catering bars around the ground are named after famous former players.

THE START OF THE MATCH

When the teams are nearly due to come out you will hear some famous classical music. This is called 'The Dance of the Knights' and it is by a composer called Prokofiev. When you hear this it means the match is going to start in a few minutes. Afternoon games usually kick off at 3.00 and end around 4.45. Evening games normally start at 7.45 and end around 9.30. Just as the teams appear the music changes from the classical music to modern pop music. Everyone cheers like mad when the teams appear so be ready to join in! The players will warm up with the mascots, then the captains will toss up to decide which end they will attack first and who will kick off and then the match gets going.

Never been to the match? Fancy going? Wonder what it's like? Find out here...

3 BUY A PROGRAMME

No visit to a match is complete without a programme – especially if it is your first ever game. A programme is the perfect souvenir of being at a particular match and it will give you loads of information about the players of both teams.

4 GO INTO THE GROUND

Your ticket has a turnstile number on it. All of the turnstiles are numbered and it's best to go in the one that has its number on your ticket because then you'll be in the right part of the ground to find your seat. However you can use just about any turnstile. If you aren't sure ask a steward or turnstile operator and they will help you.

7 HALF TIME

Each half lasts for 45 minutes plus maybe a couple of minutes' injury time. At half time the players go off for 15 minutes during which you might want to go to the toilet, get something to eat or drink or watch the half time entertainment on the pitch.

8 SECOND HALF

With a bit of luck you'll see a good game, some goals and see Sunderland win. You might be lucky and see a good game and a Sunderland win the first time you come but it is the supporters who come to every game who can be guaranteed the highs and lows of wins, draws and defeats. The important thing to learn is that being at a match is completely different to watching footy on the telly. Watching on TV means you are just watching, being at the match means you are part of the game, you can cheer the Lads on, see everything for yourself and know that you are now a Sunderland supporter... SEE YOU AT THE MATCH!

DID YOU KNOW

- Athletic Bilbao from Spain's Primera Liga wear red and white stripes because they were founded by Arthur Pentland from Sunderland?

- Ben Alnwick's dad used to be a professional kickboxer and once fought for a world title?

- Danny Collins has played cricket as well as football for Wales?

- Stephen Wright grew up as such a keen Everton supporter that he used to wear his Everton shirt under his Liverpool one when he was first training with the Reds?

- Andy Welsh was born in England and has played for Scotland at Under 19 level?

- Sunderland AFC was once called Sunderland and District Teachers' Association?

- Sunderland have won more trophies than every other English team that wears red and white stripes put together?

- No team have ever bettered Sunderland's top flight away win of 9-1 away to Newcastle United in 1908?

- Dennis Tueart, Sunderland's left winger in the 1973 FA Cup Final is now a director of Manchester City?

- Sunderland's record crowd of 75,118 is 7000 higher than that of any other club in the north east?

QUIZ ANSWERS

Have you won promotion?

The 25 questions are worth a point each. The questions are on pages 46 and 47. If you got 20 – 23 questions right you are good enough for automatic promotion. If you are really brilliant and got 24 or 25 right then you win the Championship. If you got between 15 and 19 correct then you also need to check the answers to your Play Off questions to see if you have won promotion.

GROUNDS
1) The Sunderland Stadium of Light (The Stadium of Light will do)
2) Roker Park
3) Anfield
4) Pride Park
5) The Nou Camp

NICKNAMES
1) The Black Cats
2) Sheffield United
3) Arsenal
4) Everton
5) Southampton

GOALIES
1) Ipswich Town
2) Jimmy Montgomery
3) Holland
4) Mart Poom
5) Chelsea's Peter Cech who plays for the Czech Republic

STRIKERS
1) Chris Brown (His dad is Alan Brown)
2) Stephen Elliott
3) Theo Walcott
4) Kevin Phillips
5) Anthony le Tallec

TRANSFERS
MATCH THESE PLAYERS UP WITH THE CLUBS SUNDERLAND SIGNED THEM FROM:

Rory Delap: Southampton
Stephen Wright: Liverpool
Dean Whitehead: Oxford United
Nyron Nosworthy: Gillingham
Jon Stead: Blackburn Rovers

PLAY OFF QUESTIONS
You only need to do these questions if you got between 15 and 19 points in the main quiz. You have to have got the semi final question correct for your Final answer to count. If you get both right then you win promotion.

Play Off semi final question:
Mick McCarthy

Play Off Final question:
Charlton Athletic.

CROSSWORD ANSWERS

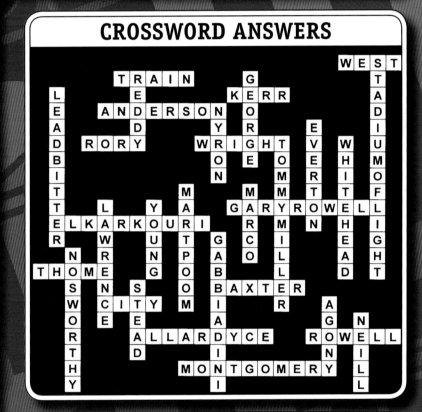

SPOT THE DIFFERENCE ANSWERS